I0755982

FINISHING LINE PRESS
www.finishinglinepress.com

THE LETTER

poems by

Greg Jensen

Finishing Line Press
Georgetown, Kentucky

THE LETTER

Copyright © 2026 by Greg Jensen
ISBN 979-8-89990-416-5 First Edition
All rights reserved under International and Pan-American Copyright Conventions. No part of this book may be reproduced in any manner whatsoever without written permission from the publisher, except in the case of brief quotations embodied in critical articles and reviews.

ACKNOWLEDGMENTS

I would like to thank my wife, Mollia, for her unstinting support.

Thank you also to Jeanne Morel, Anthony Warnke, and the Columbia City Writer's Circle for making such a welcoming space poetry in our community. This book would not exist without the encouragement of these kind souls.

Publisher: Leah Huete de Maines
Editor: Christen Kincaid
Cover Art: Greta Joy Jensen
Author Photo: Mollia Jensen
Cover Design: Elizabeth Maines McCleavy

Order online: www.finishinglinepress.com
also available on amazon.com

Author inquiries and mail orders:
Finishing Line Press
PO Box 1626
Georgetown, Kentucky 40324
USA

Contents

1 1
2 2
3 3
4 4
5 5
6 6
7 7
8 8
9 9
10 10
11 11
12 12
13 13
14 14
15 15
16 16
17 17
18 18
19 19
20 20
21 21
22 22
23 23
24 24
25 25
26 26
27 27
28 28
29 29
30 30

For Mom

1

This is the letter for which you have been waiting.
This is the letter and no other.
A letter you open in the street while rain smudges its lines, making its meaning more clear.
A letter you keep in a book for safekeeping between your favorite chapters.
You forget about the book, but the letter stays with you.
A letter that describes what it is like to be born into a world that cannot be described.
A letter you sleep with under your pillow while you dream about living a life you start to regret.
When you wake up you find yourself living a life you regret not to regret.
A letter full of bridges and tunnels and secret passages that show you the way you wouldn't have known if the letter had never arrived.
A letter full of sorrows that mean the world is a limit you keep overcoming.
A letter for you to wonder why there is this moment and no other.
A letter for you to keep pushing ahead into a flavorless future.
A letter you wouldn't have if you were nothing.
A letter addressed to the person you confuse with the person who opened the letter and started reading the words before they meant anything.
A letter you wish said more about some things and less about others.
A letter unheard of until it comes in the night and is slid under your bedroom door.
A letter written during war fought half a world away and for which the dead are remembered in its pages.
A letter you read to children who are too young to understand.
A letter you would have written if you weren't the person who needed to read it.
A letter that circles you like a satellite and unwinds your broken heart.

2

The letter is a pool of light that arrived in the house you lived in
as a child.
Rays of pure energy came over a clay horizon, through the
sliding glass door where you sat cross-legged and waited
for the day to be delivered.
In the pane you were a study of pre-adolescent contemplation.
Energy meeting energy on the same plane.
But who sent you to receive light's liquid missive?
And who would you describe it to in minute detail as if writing a
letter to the universe in its own haunted handwriting?
It took years for you to believe you were the recipient, the love of
light appearing in empty space.
What arrives more suddenly than a letter on the wings of dawn?
What can be said after you have a brush with empyrean language
in your living room before your parents can explain the
existence of non-existence?
You didn't see yourself being examined for hidden messages,
didn't even suspect you were being scrutinized by an
author whose name you would never know.

3

The letter and the world meet where the body floats in fluids and
dreams, where the body meets itself without a beginning or
end to speak of.
The letter travels networks and nodes of knowing, until it possesses
the whole of you.
Holds you in its slender ivory folds.
You want to understand the letter's inexplicable magic, to deconstruct
its vocabulary for holding power over the body it needs to
carry its secrets into the world.
The body goes where the letter goes as if delivering blood for the
purpose of sustaining awareness to the point of being
unaware.
The letter describes sickness to the body so it can understand how to
travel out of the circuit of delirium.
The letter describes love, and the body can hardly hold still long
enough for the letter to finish giving the body a deep
impression of the ways love will thrill the body, until it feels
more than the sum of its rages, griefs, and fleeting epiphanies
only to leave the body cold.
The letter puts the body on notice but doesn't tell it when to expect a
final judgment.
The heart never stops replaying the letter in its thrumming cocoon,
never unwinds the thread that connects it to the wings that
open and close in mid-air as if singing a silence the body
leaves behind.

4

Once the eagerly anticipated letter arrives, it ceases to exist.
Its handwritten confessions become a touch of smoke in the
eyes.
You rub and rub each word to feel what your body once felt
in the days and weeks before the letter was dropped in
your mailbox with a satisfying *ping*.
And still the letter is lost to you in your quest to keep it alive, to
resuscitate what it was when it was just a postmark in
Bismarck, ND.
When the letter arrived in your town, it was placed in a bag
and slung over the shoulder of an alcoholic mail
deliverer who herself was dreaming of receiving good
news on a bad day, who walked the blocks on her sturdy
legs, barely looking at the houses on her route, side-
stepping tulips and dogshit, every delivery lightening
her bag, until she was left with the burden of her own
truth weighing her down, her heart churning with
nicotine and boxed wine.
But the letter is not the story of a messenger who kills herself by
carrying what might save another.
The letter is the pulse quickening in the hours before dawn when
the envelope makes a circuitous trip without missing a
beat, finds you half-awake not knowing if today is the
day or just a cheap imitation.

5

Like you, the letter is indifferent.
It wants nothing, not even to be understood.
The letter lacks empathy, though it has traveled through sorting
machines and felt the calloused hands of dog-fearing carriers
who brought it to confess.
And yet the letter is not a criminal and has no misdeeds to disclose.
The letter doesn't even have sins of omission to declare.
Like you, the letter speaks for itself.
It crossed the country feeling alienated no matter how far to the right
or left it went.
The letter was mistakenly deposited into a ballot box but later was
rejected on the grounds it was an attempt to subvert the
dominance of those in charge.
The letter once ran for mayor but only had one signature which no
one could verify.
The letter is doing its job, despite being a cipher.
Like you, the letter contains what people want it to contain.
It comforts those who need comfort.
It breaks hearts when there is no other way.
It tells a joke to pass the time.
It feels what you feel when you are alone and wishing for someone to
say it's worth it.

6

You hold the letter over a candle and the flame dances below
sentences like an eye of a prisoner who never stops
writing appeals to his guilty verdict.
Behind the scrutiny of flame, you start to see a new pattern in
the old words.
You wipe your glasses to get a better look.
You start to feel implicated in crimes you could not have
committed.
The letter testifies not to your actions but to the impact of your
actions over time.
You are guilty of thinking you only hurt what you love without
realizing the toll indifference takes when the world turns
away from its own inhumanity.
You see through the sentences the meaning of true guilt.
Guilt is not a litany of statements one can defend or deny but an
accumulation of moments when the individual forsakes
their bond with the collective.
And these moments leave a mark that can only be seen in the
light of a low flame.
And only by those who realize they have been forsaken.
You have been forsaken like everyone else who believes they
aren't cutting off their own hands, plucking out their
own eyes.

7

The letter is for lovers who leave a trail of clothes as they rush into
bed.
The letter is the body that joins them like a third person who
translates the feeling of each touch, the sound of each cry.
Without the letter they go off in different directions, lost in carnal
confusion.
Without common language, their union is silent.
To love without a witness is to love in a dream and to feel the
beginning of a touch that never comes.
But what comes between them is more than language alone.
What comes between lovers is spelled out in a weeping of stars.
The letter is the light they describe to each other, that flies off before
they can finish.

8

Where does the letter find you?
In a hospital bed waiting for a hearing on your sanity?
You press your body into service, making it the last line of defense.
You shit on the sheets, because you refuse to be helped to the bathroom.
The doctors make courtly appearances when you least expect them.
They look on you as if you aren't hearing them correctly, so they write down your answers in order to have a complete record of your mental confusion.
Eventually, copies will be delivered to you and the court, as well as your assigned counsel in the matter of the long-winded case life has brought against you.
It will be fun to read the lies that they wrote and to argue with the judge over the meaning of the word *harm* and the means by which you have been violated over and over again.
And if the letter tells you you are free to go, it is merely another example of their lies.
How can you be free if your body continues to resist?
If the body never fails to fail, to whom are they directing their case?
You leave them nothing but the waste of a body on a white sheet.

9

The letter is a continent drifting into view.
Before you touch shore you are caught by the sense you have arrived
 at the unexplored self.
You are written into its rivers and volcanoes, making and remaking
 the earth that never stops slipping away.
There is a reason for a day that turns to dusk and becomes night all at
 once.
On dry land you know what it means to be lost once and for all, to
 be on your knees in soft sand praying there is more than a
 grand indifference to your need to put a name on the face of
 oblivion.
A face that you share just by arriving as if you and earth are one.
Are you the first to see yourself growing up in its fields, bathing in its
 alpine lakes, touching the frozen tip of an icicle?
Or is there no one behind you to go second?
Are you caught in a trap of thinking you are two people instead of
 one?
Which one is here to be discovered line by line?
The letter keeps insisting you are you even when the facts argue
 otherwise.
See what becomes of you when the sky curves into earth in order to
 make a bed for your bones.
You won't see yourself becoming a pause between coming and going,
 a breath between breaths, a space between two words that
 mean you can't even be approximate to an approximation.

10

You go on inside your life, ticking off the days, but the letter
stops you.
And if you are stopped inside of a life that continues to dream of
arriving at the place where its insignificance is finally
recognized, how do you get out?
You open the letter and read between the lines.
The difference between a good day and a bad day is one word.
At times the letter is a comfort you wouldn't trade for a better
life.
Were you the one who deserved the letter?
Or were you the one who deserved better?
The letter is silent when you ask, but that doesn't stop you from
keeping it safe.
The difference between you and everyone else is more than a
word, but none seem up to the job of telling you who
you are even in a sample sentence you could revise later.
You love being inside your life, but that doesn't mean you don't
want out.
Did the letter come to you?
Or did you come to a place in life and the letter was there behind
a small door to which you somehow had a key?
Did the letter cause you to step outside of your life, if just for
a moment, so you could taste the glue of another tongue,
hear a voice transcribe a whisper in the lobby of your
apartment building?
The difference between a letter received and a letter never sent is
a lifetime of anticipation.
You expected better than what you got.
And yet it was a whole lot better than nothing.
To be inside a life that kept you waiting.

11

And then one day you try your hand at writing back to the void that left you in its wake.
You lean in to the sheet of paper, let it catch flakes of dandruff as if you too must hide what you create.
You leave a line of blood, mucus, and sputum, each hacked out like a patient in a sanatorium.
To whom it may concern becomes your koan, the question that spoke you into existence.
Your writing is flat but enters the world going at a tilt, as if born to climb the fetid air that lingers over a dead body no one has discovered yet.
Your connection to the paper is otherworldly, though it reads like a shithouse scrawl.
When you lift your hand to massage your aching wrist, you realize you can't put your pen down.
The pointlessness is the point.
You keep heading in a direction that escapes you.
You finish a line and it wraps you in an anonymous embrace.
You feel the warmth of something you dread.
You become concerned there is no one to whom.
It's just you in a room opening up inside a moment a moment can't bear.
The threads holding you together are woven with wind.
You keep catching yourself in doorways, under the eaves of an abandoned house before rain, listening to yourself moan out of diesel-blackened tunnels.
You are a line that escapes into other lines.

12

The letter arrives from the end of history.
It tells you what you already know about the wars, the fires, the
plagues, having lived somehow through them all.
You expected worse and are disappointed at the dull finale.
You expected power to destroy itself, but power lost its edge.
You saw there was nothing at the end of history, just an ever-
widening cloud.
The cloud was whiter than paper and had no curves that could
be confused with a face that looked kind or wicked
depending on your mood.
The cloud grew no darker, never collected a bellyful of
bilgewater, though there was plenty in its mists.
The cloud didn't kill with kindness or with malice.
In fact, at the end of history nothing changed at all.
The cloud erased the line separating the beginning and the end.
Everyone expected the worst.
Everyone had a bad dream.
Everyone woke up and found there was nothing to be afraid of,
which was scarier than they expected.
The letter tells you not to worry about your children's, children's
children.
They will grow up in a never-ending cloud.
You have never seen a brighter future.

13

The letter deselects details that don't fit the narrative.
The letter tells the one thing that could be true.
But it is only true if it is excised from the body that lies with each heartbeat, fabulates a rhythm the blood taps out.
The letter is not cause or effect.
It strips life to the bone, because bones are deselected from the earth from which they emerged.
You hold the bones of the dead as if delivering a eulogy about the one thing that could be true about the bones of one body being the bones of all.
The letter is a limit to which the body is pressed.
The body learns to escape by deselecting itself from danger.
Therefore the letter is necessarily a survival story.
In order to survive, life is deselected from death.
But from what or where is death deselected?
Can one thing be true if it is taken out of the body from which it co-occurred?
A natural selection can only be valid if it includes the truth of everything that didn't fit the narrative.
You can hold the letter as long as you want, but it's only partial to what it is partial.
Bones are partial to the body as long as the body deselects itself from death.
The body is a letter that selects the details for survival.
What is not selected is implied.
Therefore death is neither selection nor deselection but the hush that surrounds the body at the beginning and end of the same story.

14

You hold the letter in your hands.
When you finish reading they aren't your hands any more.
They are your father's hands, your mother's hands.
The hands of ancestors who stole language from the gods.
You reflect on yourself being here at the end of the line, which began with an act of taking power from the almighty and making it known.
The letter is an oracle that mediates between knower and known.
Each letter, each word, each mark of punctuation steadies the void from which knowledge can be transmitted.
Your hands don't hold the contents of knowledge any more than a cardboard box holds the contents of the universe.
And yet you have read for yourself what is known about a moment in time.
And therefore you possess everything that can be grasped by the mind through a medium that escapes the mind.
And in this way you are escaping yourself by telling yourself you are here.
Who is holding the letter if not for your father and mother and ancestors who passed through the gates separating knower from known.
And who are you in this moment separate from the word and what the word holds steady.

15

The letter has a voice, but it is held in.
Like a stone in the throat.
You become someone paid to use your voice to describe how
disappointment arrives day after day.
You can't explain the origin of your speeches any more than a tree can
explain its leaves.
You are congratulated and promoted for telling people about
misfortune.
It makes you uncomfortable to use your voice to make others
question their comfort.
But you are required to get paid to ensure your family is comfortable.
Somehow you spit it out around the stone in your throat.
On your days off you go fishing for trout in the forest in faraway
creeks.
The fish hide behind rocks in the shadows before taking your lures.
You catch your limit and clean them on the shore, finding small
pebbles in their guts.
You take a string of fish home to your family and feed them what you
tempted out of darkness for the sake of their comfort.
After they are in bed and you have cleaned up the frying pan and put
away the flour and spices, you sit in the kitchen in silence.
You think about the voice you hold in all day, saying nothing.
It is not the speaker of your speeches, but a hardness inside that keeps
you from being too comfortable.
It's something you can't say to anyone, not even your wife.
It lives and dies in you without ever being tempted to show a flash of
silver scales or the white of its belly where it keeps reminders
of what gnaws at you in the night.

16

The letter arrives too late.
Everything it might have explained has already come to pass.
A stranger on the path shoulders a pickaxe and starts walking;
on his other arm he carries a bicycle tire and a tackle box.
The tools for bringing out the true story are always harder to master than you expect.
You lift up your gaze, but the horizon is already finished.
You lift up your arms and hold the emptiness of an entire evening without saying a word.
You keep digging in the falling light, replacing handfuls of dirt with handfuls of darkness until you occupy a space left by a stranger just passing through.
You light a cigarette to remind yourself that you exist, follow the red curlicues as you gesture to the silence.
All is theater, even the letter you might have read when there was daylight to follow.
The man with the pickaxe won't say if he's buried or begged the earth to return to him what used to come without asking.
The letter is preterite but tells the future by silencing the past.
You lift your tongue in your mouth and bite down on the nicotine and onions that always give you indigestion.

17

The letter arrives from no one, addressed to no one.
You begin to read with self interest.
You find yourself described as a fake, which you feel sincerely you are not.
The more details emerge about your purported charade, the more incensed you become.
You are surprised you possess so much anger, in fact.
Someone who can't possibly know you has the audacity to put forward a version of your character that doesn't remotely match the version you know.
You keep reading, hoping for a surprise ending which will make you realize all your anger was in vain.
But the letter never explains its motives, never gives you the portrait you keep inside.
Who would send a distortion knowing it would upset you?
You tear up the letter and put it in the recycling with the rest of the junk mail.
It's a relief to know you can reject all of the information used to manipulate you.
In your heart, you are someone who doesn't care what anyone thinks.
You know yourself and this fact gives you peace.
No one can take that away from you, despite this most recent lapse.
That wasn't you anyway who thought he was so mad that someone had the nerve to call him a phony.
Whoever that was didn't know you from Adam.
Whoever you are in your heart knows the truth.
Wherever you go, you are met by strangers who know nothing of you.
Whoever they are, whoever you are, there's been a big mistake.

18

Is it you reading the letter?
Are you the one who cut it open and laid it out on your desk
    where it sat holding the folded position of its travels?
Did it come to you?
Or has it been part of your life all along until now, the moment
    you realize you have been in its ken from the beginning.
Are you reading?
Or are you being read?
Are you an alphabet someone is trying to order by placing letters
    in front of silence?
Is it language you use to spell out your needs?
Or does the body tell you when it is time to eat, sleep, and fuck?
The letter has traveled through grubby hands, has been scanned
    by electronic eyes.
It has suffered every indignity to reach you.
Not once has it said a word that meant anything to someone else.
You scan the sentences looking for a clue.
Your eyes meet the text, absorbing what is written.
You take it into the same body that lusts when it learns to wait
    for the moment when it is desired equally.
The more you consume, the more greed takes over until you are
    at the feet of the letter, begging.
The body of the letter doesn't need you to be complete.
But you who are reading feel the words are for you alone.
You are read by the sounds you make lusting after a body you
    meet in the dark expecting to be laid bare.

19

The letter enters time.
Then seals itself off from time that would destroy it.
The letter owes its existence to time but refuses to observe the law of
self destruction.
You meet the letter in time, but you are on unequal footing.
The letter will go on making its case after you self-destruct.
In fact, it is only a matter of time before the letter slips out of your
fingers so you can slip back into timelessness.
Someone looks back on the letter but forgets you existed.
The letter does not create time, nor does it destroy time.
It is sad to be in time and then have it taken away.
The letter should say more about having time and having no time.
But there is not enough time for an explanation.
The letter that explained how time and timelessness coexist would
self-destruct after being read.
You keep reading anyway, as if the answer will finally be revealed.
Before long you forget you are reading.
You no longer see words on the page, though the letter is still before
you.
You curl up in bed with the letter.
When you are too tired to read any more, you slip it under your
pillow.
When you wake up you are thirty years older.
Is it sleep that proves the existence of time?
Or is sleep a pattern of forgetting your existence in time?
When you look under your pillow for the reassuring rhythm of
words, the letter has disappeared.
Have you entered timeless time?
Or have you finally self-destructed?

20

You read the letter by candlelight for the soft feathery light a
candle casts upon the page.
Each word burns in your eyes, like something you know once
before it is gone.
You hold yourself in one place, but the words refuse to sting less.
You came for truth, which you now have, guttering away.
Like the candle, the letter is a flame which casts you out.
You build yourself up, layer upon layer, for the gift of fire.
Once it touched your head you knew what there is to know of
coming and going.
Felt it burn as you touched the earth.
Felt yourself become soft and feathery.
Felt yourself cast a darkness without which you could not see.
Kept yourself arrowing a light that would falter.
Invented language for someone else to remember you by.
Cast yourself upon the page for a dying art.
Like you, the light is defenseless.
You practice being a shape for the sake of becoming a relic.
But a relic holds its shape even when buried.
The light upon the letter burns to the deepest part of you but
somehow never drives out the truth.

21

Death is a letter you read over and over.
The letter death sends is soulful, heartfelt.
You read it as if for the first time, surprised death is cruel to be kind.
Death is a perfect pen pal.
It never fails to reply even when you forget to write.
When death comes in the mail you always think it is for someone
 else.
Without regular correspondence, how would you notice death all
 around you?
How would you observe death on your breath if you didn't hold the
 letter close to your face, examining death's careful
 handwriting?
You are grateful for these helpful reminders, though they pierce you
 each time.
Death isn't trying to be a dick.
Death just wants you to remember to be ready.
When a new letter arrives, death says something different.
You read to see what has changed since death last wrote.
But you feel the same as you always do.

22

When you read the letter it starts to burn.
At first just the edges curl with small flames.
You could put them out with a slow lick of your thumb, pressing the little fire out with your fingers.
But something inside you waits to see if fire surrounding words is a gift.
You feel the heat grow in your hands.
It flashes in your face and catches the wind.
You read as fast as you can.
Some words are gone before you read them.
Some you can decipher despite the missing letters.
While the letter burns in your hands, a meaning smolders in your mind.
You stand there while a fire devours you word by word.
You start to lose pieces of yourself turned to ash.
What is the meaning of cinders?
The letter is reduced to a shadow no bigger than a thumbnail.
You try to live with a wild thought always coming for you, hunting you down.
It divides you from family and country.
It leaves no room for error.
It's just you and the slow lick of time.

23

The letter says very little.
What else could it say?
For one thing it curves away from you like a sail on a schooner going headfirst into the glittering sea.
It is not fate pushing you forward into an ever widening horizon.
It is part of you, the part you feel moving towards an object you can't see.
It depends on you to move as if in a story without end.
But fate is written as you meet the ocean and sky becoming one.
You breathe on the part of you that keeps going and where you meet an inevitable swirl.
The letter is sharper than the wind, but the wind is the only force strong enough to lift it over the horizon.
You and the letter face each other in the middle of the big, bad ocean, playing an endless game of chicken to see which of you sinks first.
The part of you that keeps going tells the story about how you stayed put while the sky moved overhead in a wheeling of stars.
The letter is the thin line that separates you from fate.
What is there but how little there is to say?
If the letter goes further than the wind, it is lost on the horizon.
If you go further than the letter, you are fated to sing alone.

24

The letter is an equation you are trying to solve.
You reduce yourself to nothing before it arrives, so you may be ready to accept the sum of its news.
The letter is not a whole number.
It is a fraction of a whole you once knew before you lost the sum in a thoughtless act.
You brought yourself back from next to nothing, living partly in one world, partly in another.
You lived in one place, but your attention scattered like smoke after a pistol that signals the start of a sprint.
You kept running between the lines, never looking to the side to see if anyone was gaining on you.
The letter was not waiting for you at the finish line to inform you of what you had just accomplished.
Your race against time meant nothing equals nothing.
You slip through a series of odd jobs: document clerk, shoe salesman, actuary, assistant to the assistant supervisor.
Each time you are told what you are worth, which sounds good on paper.
But every two weeks you see how small deductions kill your resolve.
And eventually you receive a notice from the company that cuts you loose.
And you get another chance to line up the zeroes when you go to the store for a pack of smokes.
You spend several weeks on the front porch waiting for a fraction of your pay to arrive.
It's better than nothing, which is what you were told to expect.
The letter isn't for you to figure out.
The letter is the figure you agreed to accept when you were told to get lost.

25

The letter you keep in a desk drawer under a Zippo lighter, a pair
of broken eyeglasses, expired passports, ticket stubs for
shows you swore never to forget, keys to your best
friend's house who no longer thinks of you as a friend, a
list of what it would take to finish your novel.
The letter you keep not to read but to remember what is meant
to be remembered.
Consider the wounds it brings back to the surface.
Consider the dreams it keeps stringing along.
Consider the deaths it brings back to life.
Consider what it means to have a witness who marks your
stunned appearance in time.
The people who gave you perspective, now gone.
The people who gave you their bodies, now gone.
The people who gave you their time, now gone.
The people who gave you a laugh, now gone.
The people who gave you praise, now gone.
The people who gave you a good word, now gone.
The people who gave up on you, now gone.
The letter you couldn't not forget.
To be someone a witness struggles to recall.
To be the subject of all subjectivity.

26

Letters are meant to be eaten, preferably in one sitting.
Some letters are nourishing to the mind and make you forget your
small life after you have digested them.
Some letters flood the heart until it is drowning in sad-happy feelings.
Some letters feed the body alone, giving it supernatural powers that
allow you to leave home and join the circus.
Once you received a letter that fed you for a week.
Each morning you ate a page and felt full for the rest of the day.
At the end of the week you stopped eating, feeling like you had lost
the love of your life.
You had no appetite for the foolishness that kept coming to your
mailbox.
You had already eaten enough for a lifetime.
You stayed in bed remembering the letter that was your daily bread.
Your neighbors grew worried and called the police to check on you.
Eventually you received a letter that compelled you to court to
explain your unwillingness to continue your small life.
After your testimony, you were presented with a court order that told
you you had no choice but to eat and live.
When you got home, you felt better that people cared about you
enough to write that you must go on.
You never had the same appetite you once did.
But when a letter came, you forced yourself to open it up and take a
bite, even a small nibble, a sentence or two, to remind you of
the one that came and filled up your small life.

27

In the letter a voice.
In the voice a recognition.
In the recognition a feeling of floating.
In the feeling of floating a seed.
In the seed a map.
On the map a circumference.
On the circumference a scrap of land.
On the scrap of land a garden.
In the garden a code.
In the code the riddle of existence.
In the riddle of existence shovelfuls of soil.
In the shovel a force.
In the force a denial.
In the denial a death.
In the death a rebirth.
In the rebirth a death.
In the denial a force.
In the force a shovel.
In shovelfuls of soil the riddle of existence.
In the riddle of existence a code.
In the code a garden.
In the garden a scrap of land.
On the scrap of land a circumference.
On the circumference a map
On the map a seed.
In the seed a feeling of floating.
In the feeling of floating a recognition.
In the recognition a voice.
In the voice a letter.

28

Your letter is lost.
You try writing the post office and imagine your note being opened
    and stared at by a face used to getting unpleasant news.
A face creased by years of holding the stub of a cigar on one side of
    his mouth and not caring what anyone thinks.
These are the sorts of faces that hold the fate of your letter and the
    letters of all people waiting for news of the world.
To be delivered out of hopelessness, you must believe in the hands
    that carry news of the world, home by home, as if each one is
    receiving exactly what they have been waiting for all their
    lives.
When a letter is lost, hope doubles down.
Bets against fate are never paid.
But that doesn't stop anyone from testing their story when it has
    slipped away.
You wait for the letter, like a colonel waiting for news of his great
    reward that recognizes the sacrifices he made for his country
    in battle.
You and the colonel stare at your breakfast of huevos rancheros and
    feel a new day coming sunny side up.
The letter arrives by not arriving.
The news for you and the colonel is clear because it doesn't exist.
You are not forgotten because you are not remembered.

29

The orientation of sky to earth.
The orientation of breath to body.
The orientation of word to paper.
The orientation of the eye to the line.
The orientation of meaninglessness to meaning.
The orientation of death to life.
The orientation of the reader to the letter.
Where paper meets the sky, squaring itself with the horizon.
Over which all can be seen.
In whom sky and earth are one.
In whom breath and body coexist.
In whom word and paper interpenetrate.
In whom the eye and the line are focused.
In whom meaning is made out of meaninglessness.
In whom death is a manifestation of life.
In whom the sky and horizon meet.
In whom the letter is born.

30

You leave the letter for someone else to read after you're gone.
It's magic.
But it's not magic.
You wave your hand over your body and "Poof!" you're still there.
The letter is proof you never left.
You hide behind the door and watch someone pick up where you left off.
They read with self-interest about someone who became no one.
They see themselves getting caught up in your diminishing story.
You see them wave their hand over the letter to prove they are still there.
When they get to the part where you are saying goodbye, they are already crying.
A bug ugly cry.
They wave their hand over the letter to prove they are still there.
They leave the letter for the next someone to pick up where they left off.
They join you behind the door.
It's magic.
But it's not magic.
There are two of you in the room.
But only one of you is there.
The letter is proof you never left.
You keep saying goodbye to someone who picks up where you left off.
How many of you can fit in the room hiding behind the door?
The letter is silent, but you leave it for someone to read after you're gone.
"Poof!"

Greg Jensen has spent 30 years working with individuals experiencing homelessness, mental illness and addiction. His poetry has appeared in *december, Bear Review, Crab Creek Review, Rabid Oak, and Porridge Magazine.* Greg lives in Seattle, WA, and holds an MFA in Poetry from Pacific University.

www.ingramcontent.com/pod-product-compliance
Lightning Source LLC
LaVergne TN
LVHW090540110826
845146LV00003B/1198

* 9 7 9 8 8 9 9 9 0 4 1 6 5 *